The
Day
I Shot
Cupid

voice

Hyperion   New York

Jennifer Love Hewitt

The Day

I
Shot

Cupid

Hello, My Name Is Jennifer Love Hewitt
and I'm a Love-aholic

Library of Congress Cataloging-in-Publication Data

Hewitt, Jennifer Love

   The day I shot Cupid : hello, my name is Jennifer Love Hewitt and I'm a love-aholic / Jennifer Love Hewitt.

        p. cm.

   ISBN 978-1-4013-4112-1

   1. Dating (Social customs) 2. Man-woman relationships. 3. Single people. I. Title.

   HQ801.H4735 2010

   306.70973'090511–dc22   2009048173

FIRST EDITION

Designed by Janet M. Evans

10 9 8 7 6 5 4 3 2 1

SUSTAINABLE FORESTRY INITIATIVE — Certified Fiber Sourcing — www.sfiprogram.org

THIS LABEL APPLIES TO TEXT STOCK

We try to produce the most beautiful books possible, and we are also extremely concerned about the impact of our manufacturing process on the forests of the world and the environment as a whole. Accordingly, we have made sure that all of the paper we use has been certified as coming from forests that are managed to ensure the protection of the people and wildlife dependent upon them.

This book is dedicated to all of you looking for love. Mom, G-ma, Michelle, Jenny, and Dye, who always teach me about who I want to be. My girlfriends, who are always there. My brother, who is my hero. Scott, for believing in my book. And JK, for being a great partner and my real truth. I love you . . .

❧ Contents ❧

**BREAKING UP IS EASY TO DO;
SURVIVING IT IS THE HARD PART**
*(Can't Live With 'Em, Can't Live Without 'Em,
Can't Shoot 'Em! Well, Maybe in Some States.)*

FOR FEMALE EYES ONLY

The
Day
I Shot
Cupid

Preface

Okay, so why did I, an actress in her thirties, decide to write a book on dating? Well, leave it to Cabo Wabo! I had a massive broken heart, so I hopped on the plane with my mom, aunt, and a bunch of friends. We found ourselves at this beautiful home overlooking the ocean and, like most meetings of the female brain, talking about men. I was so intrigued, the age groups, types of women, and lifestyles were all so different, but the message and moments the same. Dating is hilarious and awkward as hell. Relationships are difficult, beautiful, and confusing. And love is somehow worth it all. It was like the pen and paper had to be used at that moment, so I took all the things we were talking about and started writing. Of course, I added my own funny comments to them, because if you can't laugh you won't make it.

At dinner that night I presented my romance thought pages to the table, hoping to ease any past pain, laugh about the hours of life lost on bad dates, and show that we are all the same. They loved it (the tequila helped)! As I wrote them, healing began for me as well.

At the end of our great trip, I went home with a new thought. What if this is why I went through all my dating crap? Maybe I'm supposed to be the kindred spirit of millions of women out there who are just like me. And there it was, the new relationship that I would begin would be with me, my past, my present, my laughter, my pain, and, most important, all of you.

Jennifer Love Hewitt

Introduction

This, for me, is the perfect place to start. Although I was actually born on February 21, there was a chance that I would come one week earlier, on February 14. That's right, Valentine's Day. I refused to believe until I was ten or eleven years old that Valentine's Day was not actually created for me. Why? Because my name is Love! My mom named me Love and almost gave birth to me on Valentine's Day. Hello? I was born to be a hopeless romantic. It's worked well for me so far, or so I thought. And that brings us to now. This is the most eye-opening and slightly depressing part of the book, so let's get it over with. What I am about to tell you will include shocking details, lies, and murder. Continue to read at your own risk.

Okay, here it goes. On a cold day, with a little rain falling on the windows (who am I, Agatha Christie?), in the most gorgeous light of the afternoon, I sat at my computer, wondering what I could say today that would have some real value to those of you kind enough to read this book. I decided to turn to my faithful friend Cupid for some help. You know, Cupid (said with little kid voice)—cute little guy, kind of like a baby and a man all in one. The little man in the diaper who finds us true love, shoots our dream man with an arrow, brings him to us, plays the violin, and helps us live happily ever after. That Cupid. (Back in my own voice.) What I found next would forever change me. What the hell to my Googling Cupid eyes should appear, but the TRUTH!!!!!!!!!!!!!!!!!!!!!!!!

Cupid was actually a scorned lover. A person so hurt that he made poison arrows to shoot at people that would hopefully destroy their chance for love, because misery loves the

Jennifer Love Hewitt

company of a tiny man in diapers. He was an evil little shit, not a cute baby with magic arrows waiting to point at our perfect companion and bring us love's every happiness. Lock your doors. Cupid is not a good guy! Suddenly my love life flashed before my eyes: all the Valentine's Days, the arrows I shot in my mind toward the dream guy in front of me, the hours I spent thinking Cupid would make it better. And for what? He was just as depressed and hurt as I was. And P.S.—he didn't want to use his powers for good. It begs the thought—we saw a little man in a diaper shooting arrows and thought that meant true love?????

After an hour of seriously doubting my stock in Hallmark, I knew exactly what I had to do. I HAD TO SHOOT CUPID!! I had to believe in my mind that there could be romance without him. Maybe not the kind with symphonies and floating hearts (although that kind stabbed me in the back more than a few times), but something I could create with another person that would be all our own. Romantic

The Day I Shot Cupid

comedies are there to give us dreams and butterflies, but what we can create in our own lives could be not only better but real.

So I did it! I SHOT HIM! This would always be . . . THE DAY I SHOT CUPID. I let my mind kill all its previous romantic ideas and believe what would come next would be greater.

As I write this, I am only two weeks into this "transformation." I'm not gonna lie, I have had a few "everything is changing" panic attacks, but I also feel like I'm on the brink of real growth. I ask myself now what romance really is to me. What a man needs to do and what I would want to do for him. I am learning, and not depressed by the way, how to create my own fireworks and rapid heartbeat. I'm suddenly not as let down by everyday romantic screwups because the only thing to live up to is organic, from within, not a list of do's and don'ts given to me by romantic icons who aren't real. At first glance you may be thinking . . . Jaded? Bitter? Hurt too much? But let's change

Jennifer Love Hewitt

those thoughts to something more productive, like Strong, Realistic, and Grown-Up. Let's never again rely on someone or some myth to bring us happiness or love. Let's try it ourselves. Let's make our own paths and believe that what the universe has for us is perfect. Let's go out and find the love we always wanted but this time with our feet planted on the ground, our inner sparkle as the arrows, and the belief that love does happen for all of us. By the way, if you see a man in diapers, keep walking!

The Day I Shot Cupid

It was important for me to tell my views of men *and* women so that you know I take no sides. I really do think both sexes are completely nuts and beautiful. We will always need and want each other. It is just all about communication, understanding, and, oh yeah, knowing when to say you're sorry, even when you're right.

Let's Talk

Men,

Women,

and
Where

We Are

A kiss is a lovely trick designed by nature to stop speech when words become superfluous.

—*Ingrid Bergman*

Cereal Dater

(and not Cocoa Puffs)

*S*erial dater—it's like a bad KICK ME sign on my back. It's not a cute little nickname my girlfriends gave me for laughs. It's a nickname given to me at least a thousand times in major magazines, television shows, and articles that are supposed to be talking about my work. And, oh yeah, the people who said it DON'T KNOW ME! I cannot even tell you how many times I've been reading an article, happy with what they have written, focusing on all the right things, and then, like the clap, it appears, *serial dater*. The term I have come to be permanently perplexed by.

What does it mean? That I date men and kill them? Yes, I have dated a lot, not on purpose, by the way. I would have loved to have met my soul mate in fourth grade and never looked back. Not my fate obviously. So, I have dated, not any different from anyone else, except my entire dating history has been documented by the press. So I ask only this: please wipe *serial dater* off the books and think of me as a girl who is looking for love just like you.

The Day I Shot Cupid

Balls, a Dress, or a Dress That Hides Our Balls

will never forget the time a guy I was seeing told me to leave my balls at home before our date. I didn't understand what he meant. When he explained, it made sense. I was trying to control our dates like business meetings, moving too fast, as if I had an agenda to get through and couldn't talk about anything else but work (okay, I still had a lot of growing up to do). It's true, during the day, for my career, business, and personal strength, in essence I strap a pair on as armor, but then at night, I want to be soft, girly, and taken care of. Although I understood what he meant, I was insulted. Why can't there be four balls in a relationship and two of them be mine? Then, after the silent treatment, kicking him a thousand times in my mind and a movie, I realized something: My theoretical balls were taking away his chance to be the guy. He wanted to step up and let me be the girl I so wanted to be, but my balls were blocking the way. I had to be willing to be the softer, not so feisty version of myself to get what he and I both wanted. Ah, such a nice thought . . . for about a week.

QUESTION: Why can't we be strong, self-assured, tough, sometimes even scrappy, and still be treated like a girl? Or . . . why don't we choose the men who will let us be that? Which brought me to my big question: WHAT DO WE WANT? THE BALLS, THE DRESS, OR THE DRESS THAT HIDES OUR BALLS?

To be honest, I still go back and forth. Every time I watch an old movie I want to be the damsel in distress in a dress (think King Kong and Jessica Lange). Every time I watch a Julia Roberts movie I want the dress *and* balls (oh

The Day I Shot Cupid

yeah, I'm talking about *Pretty Woman*). Every time I watch *Oprah* I just want a big pair. Sometimes I'm great at being a girl and other times I find myself playing his part and mine. But I am making a decision right here and now. I think hiding all of that power under a knock-out Miu Miu sundress is the way to go!

What we forget is every one of us is great just because of who we are. If you feel strong, you will be strong. We have curves that make even the greatest designers' clothes look better (even though they usually show them on sticks). When our hair blows the right way in the wind we can stop traffic. We glow when they sweat. We can do a hundred and fifty things at once and, oh yeah, bleed every month. And on our best day we are the one thing that can leave a man speechless. So be strong, have personal power—good God, roar if you have to! But a couple of nights a week try letting it all be your undergarment and on top put a dress, perfume, some sparkle powder, and a little willingness to let him lead.

Jennifer Love Hewitt

You come to love not by finding
the perfect person, but by seeing
an imperfect person perfectly.

—Sam Keen

Macho, Metro, or Hero

(and then there were three · · · types, that is)

THE MACHO MAN

He plays lots of sports, worships his guy friends, loves beer, and is always planning an adventure that has you dangling from ropes. He will never be as sensitive as you want. He's the brawny guy, super strong, who makes you feel protected. He has strong lips and makes you remember the guys you dreamed of when you were eight.

THE METROSEXUAL

Oh dear God! He's the guy none of us ever pictured. Metrosexual? What does that even mean?! Who knew it would be okay for your boyfriend to have as many hair products as you, order diet Coke while you order regular, spend more than you do on the finest fabrics, and take all your tissues at the hot romantic comedy. They are sensitive, aware of your feelings, and fulfill the more yin-yang needs in your relationship (they can also be one parking spot over from your gay best friend).

THE HERO

He is a gentleman who opens your door and knows the importance of a flower. He is not afraid to let you see him cry, plans dates for you when you least expect it, still believes in a good love letter, can admit that he has watched you sleep, and dresses up for you so you feel like the luckiest girl in the room. He wants to understand what romance means to you and make it happen. He lets you be strong and loves when you are weak. He is the one you wait for and think you will never find. And sometimes, sadly, he is the one in front of us who we miss.

The good news is none of these are bad choices. The bad news is we kind of want parts of all three. So how do we get that? If I knew, I would be the eighth wonder of the world! Maybe, for now, we should open our minds, let down our defenses, and try to see it from their side. Women are very complicated—I say this part carefully—maybe it's not always the guy's fault. There is someone out there for all of us, I really do believe that. But instead of looking

Jennifer Love Hewitt

for perfection, look for happiness, because remember, as women, we can also get it wrong.
And our so-called perfect mirror can be turned
on us at any moment and, oh God, we do not
want to see that! Let's look at each other with
love and respect and find the one who is right
for us, not the one who is perfect.

The Day I Shot Cupid

Dumbfounded Genitals, or Who Took My Mojo?

Just when we think guys don't think of us, they do. Except it's not how wonderful or complex we are. They think, "What'd I do now?" Or "Will I ever make her happy?" Kind of sweet, right? Or are they just lost and ready to give up? I've talked to some guys, and until the girl figures out her woman, the boy can't figure out his man. OLD SCHOOL VS. NEW SCHOOL seems to be their biggest complaint.

Old-School PHONE CALL

When a guy asked for your phone number and just couldn't wait until the next day to call, he was peachy, dreamy, and so cute! If a guy asked for your number and waited to call, he was shy or respectful. You would sweat with excitement and anticipation!

New-School PHONE CALL

If a guy calls the next day, he's desperate, hard up, or a stalker. If he waits a while to call, he's a player, man-whoring himself out to skanks, or "he's just not that into you."

P.S. Now that I know he's just not that into me, where do I go from there? Yeah, thanks for that advice.

Old-School DINNER

A woman would maybe offer to go dutch for dinner (that means each pays half). But most of the time she would never even think of paying and would be grateful that a nice young man had treated her to dinner.

New-School DINNER

If a guy suggests going dutch, he's a moocher, broke, using you, and probably won't get to date number two. If he pays sometimes, you thank him. But other times, it's "Why? You don't think I can pay for dinner? I have a job. I'm not your little woman."

Jennifer Love Hewitt

Old-School ROMANCE

If a guy was romantic or made a fool of himself for love, he was husband material, well raised, and the one you had been looking for.

New-School ROMANCE

If a guy is too romantic or makes a fool of himself for love, it's "Did you cheat on me? Is that why you're being so nice? Are you gay? Are you a stalker? Or, I know, you just want in my pants!"

Now, although these examples are extreme and do not represent all women, they do happen and we do seem that crazy to guys. So maybe we should step back and think for a minute. Have we gone too far? Is it necessary to fight so hard when it comes to love? Are we

The Day I Shot Cupid

so used to fighting for our position as women that we don't know when to quit? And here's the big one: Are we risking our chance at being the girl? Guys are lost and need our help. We have to decide what we want and how we want it in order for them to give it to us. We have to be clear and decisive (some of us may have to look up the definitions of *clear* and *decisive*). So here is something to try. Before you go out with him the next time, make a decision about who you are as a woman in love. Do you want to be the girl? Do you want to be the boss? Or do you want to be his equal (remember that whole dress that hides our balls thing)? And you also have to decide if you want a man who is just trying to please you, a man who is scared, or a man who is being himself. Once you decide, stick to it. Show him in words or actions—your choice—what kind of man your woman needs.

If you want to be the girl, then fight hard all day, be a pit bull, whatever, but when he picks you up or gets home, melt into his arms and

Jennifer Love Hewitt

make him think he can take care of everything. Show him Hugh Grant movies (so he can learn some modern-day romance moves). Let him open the door. Let him be himself. Don't be weak, but let him be the hero. He might just become the man you want.

If you want to be the boss, then go out and find someone who is confident enough in himself to handle your strong woman. Let him know that sometimes you want to call the shots and don't complain if he lets you. It's your world, little miss bossy, he just lives in it.

If you want to be his equal, then explain it to him. You want romance, but you don't want to lose your power. You want to pay for dinner sometimes, but you also want him to surprise you. You don't want him to do things for you; you want him to do things with you.

I'm not saying this will cure all in the dating world, but if men and women would tell each other some of the things they tell their friends, it would be more honest and maybe more of the relationship we are looking for. Don't get

The Day I Shot Cupid

me wrong, some guys (and some women for that matter) will just never get it. But some, with a little help, just might. I think life and love can be what you make them. Figure out what *you* want out of love and life and go get it. If your guy or girl doesn't fit those things, then find someone who will. We can no longer assume men know what we want; they don't. So instead of fighting only for ourselves, maybe love is fighting for each other. And maybe real love is something we shouldn't have to fight so damn hard for.

Jennifer Love Hewitt

Flossed and Tossed

It's 9:45 and I'm getting dressed for my day, but it's different now. I'm stressed about my G-string. I think about putting my granny panties on (sorry, Grandma), saved only for laundry day, then something comes over me. As Sisqó's "Thong Song" plays on the radio behind me, I start to think about the young girls at Rancho Bernardo High, April 26, 2002. They were asked to lift their dresses before they entered the dance. The principal at the high school asked the girls who arrived at the dance what kind of undies they were wearing. The female counselor lined up the girls against the wall and did an undie check. One of the girls said, "We were in front of the entire class, the counselor, assistant principal, and two campus cops." If the girls had on a thong they were turned away. **QUESTION:** Where did those school officials buy their crack? What did they think they were protecting? Talk about missing the forest for the trees!

FACT: Price of a cheap G-string, eight bucks. Price of an expensive G-string, one hundred. A young girl's dignity, priceless. Bottom line, there is nothing redeeming in this story. School dances used to be first kisses and the running man. Now it's gang shootings and panty checks?? Something to think about—no boys were checked for boxers or briefs. Still in my closet with Sisqó, I declare today G-string day! To the young girls at Rancho Bernardo High, I am so sorry you had to deal with such humiliation. And to the school officials, don't knock a G-string until you try one!

Jennifer Love Hewitt

I want you to know you are not alone. I have experienced, laughed at, cried about, and had done to me all the things you are about to read. I have loved dating and hated it. I have known great men and not so great men. But the trenches of dating have taught me what I want and don't want. Who I am and who I want to be. We must all go through it, and without it, what would we talk about over cocktails?!

The Things We Are Faced with While

Dating

and in

Relationships

(The Hookups, the Big Ups, and the Big Downs)

In real love you want the other person's good. In romantic love you want the other person.

—Margaret Anderson

The Stages Are Set

- The Eye Contact
- The Flirt
- The First Drink
- The Text
- The First Date
- The First D and M
  (Deep and Meaningful)
- The Great Sex
- The Boyfriend/Girlfriend
- The Spoon

39

The Day I Shot Cupid

THE EYE CONTACT

his is the first moment. For women, it's where the sun shines, the clouds part, butterflies start to flutter, and there's a small chance that your entire future might start tonight. For men, I've been told, it's the first thing they notice. It's called "putting it out there." Your eyes say it all: "Hello, I'm goin' home with you" or "You're goin' home with me." "I'm the one you want, so stop looking." Sometimes the eyes just say, "Let's dance!" or " Buy me a drink!" Or they can say the unfortunate, "I'm terrified, oh God, he doesn't know I'm looking at the guy behind him." Be very cautious, ladies, when you give that first look. It tells what kind of girl you are and what kind of girl you want to be. Whether you go classic or smoky, the eyes are the windows to the soul, so work it!

Jennifer Love Hewitt

THE FLIRT

his next step is where boys become men. "Is your father a thief? Because he stole the stars and put them in your eyes" is *not* what we want to hear. Or, my favorite, and the night I will never forget, when I dressed up, waited all night for a guy to talk to me, and got "that guy." He asked me if I was Irish because his penis was "Dublin." I didn't date or go out for five months after that. If those are my choices, I'm good for now. The flirt is as important as the first night of sex because it tells us whether or not you will even be able to give us a first night of sex. You have to be smooth, but not slick; warm, but not aggressive; interesting, but not pompous—and humor is always the key. Just talk to us, no tricks, all personality. And, oh yeah, don't be seen talking to every girl in the bar before us. If they didn't want it, we don't either.

The Day I Shot Cupid

THE FIRST DRINK

This drink can tell you a lot. If he has eight, bad sign. If he has a Cosmo and you have a scotch, it could also be a bad sign. If he gets angry with alcohol, really bad sign. But if he can give great conversation, gets fun or sexy with alcohol, wants to tell you how beautiful you are, and it's effortless, congrats, you are moving on to the next drink and the next step.

42

THE TEXT

This is just fun! You can say whatever you want and put it all out there. He can make your heart race with four smileys and the right words. But beware: don't let it go too far or for too long. Be coy and move him quickly to some face-to-face time.

Jennifer Love Hewitt

THE FIRST DATE

he eye contact, the flirt, the first drink, and the text all got you right here. Both of you in your best outfits, trying not only to impress, but be impressed. You are telling all your best stories; he is showing all his best traits. The wine is amazing, the lighting perfect, the food, who cares? And his eyes are even more beautiful than you remembered. If all goes perfectly, he will call you tomorrow and you will wake your girlfriends up with details when you get home.

THE FIRST D AND M
(Deep and Meaningful)

his is a very important conversation. Not for the reasons you may think. It's because women make a mistake in the first d and m, and believe me they pay later. We are so willing to give ourselves over to love and the good feelings that come with it that our ears fail us. We shut off every clue men give us to who they really are and instead plug into those spaces who we want them to be and what we thought they said. Really, I can't express this enough, listen to what they say, EVERYTHING! It's telling you who they will be in a relationship within six months—that's a lot of time you could save.

THE GREAT SEX

*O*h God! This gets us every time. "The First Time." Yes, it's a bigger deal for us than it is for them, blah, blah, blah, but how good the act feels matters to both. When it works, it's amazing. The horizontal lambada can change any bad day into a good one, end fights, and move two people into the next phase. Now, this is a little old-fashioned, but girls, know who you are giving it to. If you want a relationship with a guy, show him what kind of woman you are. If he can get it the first night and you're too drunk to remember, what does he have to come back for? On the flip side, men have to have a sexual connection to invest, so don't hold out too long (unless, of course, that's your belief or agreement with your guy). And one more thing: it doesn't always have to be so serious; it's okay to just have great sex. But remember, your body is a temple, not a 7-Eleven; you decide when it's open and who gets to come in. And guys, sexual relationships can be stormy, so wear a raincoat.

45

THE BOYFRIEND/GIRLFRIEND

his part isn't so easy. This is where two different people with two different lives have to make it work. I'm not saying that all the fun stuff ends—by the way, if it does, you're not in the right twosome. I just mean this is where, if a person or a relationship is worth it, you do the work to make it last.

You want to be in something that brings out the best in you—where you can be your true self. You want to be with someone who makes you laugh, who is sexy, romantic, and knows what you are worth. Respect and trust are essential. I have struggled with the trust issue in my life. It's hurt my personal growth, as well as growth in my relationships, and truly, most of the time, it comes more from my own fear of getting hurt than the other person's actions. So don't make my mistakes, and just trust as much as you can. And respect—this one is hard because it has to be earned, reciprocated, and kept. By that I mean your partner has to be respectful of you also, and has to always act in a way that doesn't damage your respect for them. We've all had breakups, but the worst ones are when someone not only hurts you, but does it in a way that makes you lose respect for them. And last, I will say this: a really good

Jennifer Love Hewitt

relationship is where both people can learn from each other, the person you love can make you a better version of yourself, and you can do the same for them.

THE SPOON

I'm a spooner, I love to spoon!" There, I said it. This is one of the top BF/GF perks. Like a Velcro monkey, I will suck to the back of my cuddle partner, creating the ultimate spoon. But—and it's no secret—guys hate to spoon. They prefer to fork, lol! Like a little, soft, female electric blanket, we cause them to sweat, they try to breathe through our long hair, and they almost always end up clinging to one side of the bed like a cliff that can only bring them death. So here's the trick: Play it cool until he falls asleep and then Velcro yourself to him, quickly and with very little motion (think Tom Cruise in *Mission: Impossible*). And then, if and when he wakes, turn

The Day I Shot Cupid

quickly, like you were just stretching, and wait. When the little lamb sleeps again One . . . Two . . . Three . . . Velcro!!!!!!!!!!!!!

THE REAL PERSONALITY

I don't wish this next step on anyone and some can avoid it. Remember when I said to really listen to everything he says early on? This is why. If, suddenly, six months in, he has anger issues, an inclination to be overly flirtatious with other girls, or is selfish or rude in the way he speaks to you, girls, please don't hate me, but that's your fault. People can learn things in their relationships to make the other person more comfortable and make small adjustments in personality, but really, leopards don't change their spots. He probably told you in his own way, or showed you those behaviors six months ago, while you were dressing him up in your mind in a Prince Charming outfit, white horse included, and his

48

Jennifer Love Hewitt

words were drowned out by the *Bridget Jones* soundtrack in your head. What we do in falling in love is not wrong; it's just not in our best interest. We turn them into what we want instead of seeing what they are, and we should keep looking until we find the guy who really is all the things we want. Or, maybe, along the way, just really listen, look inside, and see if those qualities are worth moving ahead with. And, oh yeah, there will never be perfect, but there *will* be pretty great. And a relationship in which people are really listening sounds pretty great to me!

THE TOILETRY KIT

*O*MG, *let me just embarrass myself right now.* I spent three hours once making his and her toiletry kits. One for my house and one for his house. At the time, I thought it was the most amazing gift. When I presented them I thought I would receive the Greatest

Romantic Award. Uh, not what happened. Instead, I received awkward silence, followed by more awkward smiles, and never heard from him again. My advice, use overnight bags for as long as it takes. And when he is ready to put stuff at yours, still wait, and even then, start with small things and let him lead. Trust me, I know.

THE PARENTS

m, have you watched Jerry Springer? When has it ever gone smoothly meeting the parents? There is always either awkward him, awkward you, awkward them, or awkward us. Awkward him is him hoping that they don't bring up every ex-girlfriend and dorky *Star Trek* high school photo. Awkward you is hoping you wore the right thing, aren't allergic to his mom's cooking, and don't get felt up by his weird uncle. Awkward them

Jennifer Love Hewitt

is their very vocal doubt about whether this will last, not even knowing he had a girlfriend, or calling you by the last one's name. Awkward us is the silence . . . in your still Strawberry Shortcake–decorated bedroom. They could be your in-laws if you go to the next level. Will you go to the next level? And can you have intimacy in a Strawberry Shortcake bedroom? I honestly have no advice on how to make this easier, but I do send you into battle with love.

THE DENIAL

*A*fter you meet the parents, guys go into a phase of trying to pretend that the relationship isn't moving into a serious place, that it's still just casual dating with toiletry kits, sleeping together every night, and meeting the parents. This is when women have to be very careful and very smart. You actually want him to think it's no big deal because you don't want him to get scared, but you also want him to know that you're the type of girl he should commit to. Not that I'm a fan of games, but kick your game into high gear! Always look amazing. Really try to pick your battles. Try to be unpredictable and sometimes unavailable. Give him more sex than he asks for. If he works late or has to cancel on something say, "Okay." Show him how easy it is to be in a serious relationship with you and still live his life. That two can in fact be better than one. Don't lie or turn into someone you're not, just look at the relationship and him as no serious thing. In return, he will look at you seriously. Once a man has decided he can commit to you and not lose himself, when he knows you are "the one," the chemistry in his body and mind will change, and seeing you the way you've always wanted him to will be inevitable. So go ahead, be the Queen of Denial.

Jennifer Love Hewitt

THE "ARE WE?"

*O*ne morning it will all just be different. Something, some moment, will change the dynamic. It could be something he says or a look in his eye. It might be the way she sleeps or knows how to give you space when you need it. But both of you will just wonder, are we? Are we really going to do this? Be together always? Sleep only with each other? Make a family? Is this it?

And the answer will be exactly what you both wanted. All the dating drama, little fights, getting to know each other's quirks, insecurities, and questions will be over (at least for this phase). You will both just be. A sigh of relief will come over you and you will be on your way to what will hopefully be a beautiful future. Congrats.

53

THE "WE ARE"

*A*nd then there were two. *Now that you* have said good-bye to dating, worked out the relationship do's and don'ts, and find yourself in commitment bliss, the mind starts asking the next question: Will he ask me to marry him? When? Your friends begin to wonder and you can't help but start sending little hints to your guy. Where is *his* mind? Well, there are a few possibilities: (a) Not even thinking about marriage, sorry but it's the truth; (b) thinking about it and wanting it, but thinking he still has time before he has to do it (that's men, it's okay, you want him to really be ready); or (c) planning the most beautiful surprise of your life and making you squirm. (We all hope for this option.)

MY ADVICE IS SIMPLE: Don't let other people tell you how or when it's supposed to happen. It's your relationship and you want it to be organic and real. Don't push him. A man pushed into marriage or babies is a caged animal ready

Jennifer Love Hewitt

to attack. And then you will never know if he really wanted to or was just tired of hearing about it. And, most important, daydream about the moment, but remember how powerful the imagination can be. It won't be a Julia Roberts movie because that's not real. It won't be a fairy tale because that's also not real. It will just be your man asking his woman to be his wife. And it will be magical because he's a man making a real commitment that goes beyond his instincts because you have inspired him to do so. This moment, for him, is all the romance he's got. He has thought, planned, and sweated getting ready to do this. Let it be more perfect than a movie or something in your mind because it's real and it's beautiful.

THE RING

Oh God, I can't even breathe when I talk about it. It's like the world has all the sound sucked out of it and everything's in slow motion except for your heart. As that little box opens, so do your dreams, and there it is, the Ring. There are two scenarios with this:

 The "Oh my God, it's the biggest thing I've ever seen, where did he get the money? Who cares, he's mine, it's mine, and all of my friends will be jealous" scenario.

OR

The "Keep smiling, it's tiny, not the cut we talked about, he makes more money than that, I care, he doesn't know me" scenario.

Both exist and we have no control over which one will happen—or do we? This is embarrassing and personal, but once a month, since I was twelve years old, I go to my favorite jewelry store and try on my dream ring. Some

Jennifer Love Hewitt

might say pathetic, I say prepared. While you get a "take a chance" ring, I will be blinging it all day with my "dream ring." And actually, in the last few months or so, trying to be more prepared, I have found three rings that would make my heart stop. So if my guy ever starts putting out the "ring vibe" he will have choices, but they will be choices I love. I don't apologize. A woman's engagement ring is like a man's dream car, it's what we wear every day, what people ask to see first after the announcement, and whether we want to admit it or not, it says a lot about what our man knows about and thinks of us. A friend of mine wasn't so happy with her engagement ring, and so, after a few months, she traded up and got a bigger one. It was a big deal between the two of them and could have been avoided with a little bling preparation.

Also, men will know they've done a good job based on how much she wears it. If it's always in the soap dish, jewelry box, or not on when company's over, she's not crazy about the ring. Don't get me wrong, the ring is still about the meaning behind it, but there is also bling vanity, I'm not gonna lie. So here's a thought: start looking for what you love, and narrow it down to three rings. When it's that time in the relationship, show them to your guy and help him understand what it means to you and why. He wants to make you happy, and trust me, guys will love the help. And then know that when he opens that box, one of the three things you love will be in there. And then you can have the "Oh my God, I knew he would pick that one, it's perfect, he is amazing, he's going to be my husband, and thank you JLH" scenario!

THE ENGAGED

his is where my knowledge ends. I have not gone past the engagement, but I did learn something while I was engaged. It's as beautiful as it should be. It is a time for flowers, parties, congrats, planning, dreaming, and contentment. But it's also a time for reflection. It's a time to really look at yourself and your partner, individually and together, and have respect for where you're headed. Take care of any issues or problems in this phase because in marriage they will only get bigger. Know that your views are compatible on all the major issues, such as children, family, fidelity, religion, and commitment. Even though the stats right now aren't favorable for marriage doesn't mean that you can't change it. Just be ready. Know that marriage is a responsibility and will take work, but it's beautiful when done right. So while you're engaged, have fun and take a million memory photos to remember this time. But also slow everything down and truly understand and appreciate the next step you will take. As you leave all of us single ladies behind to find our perfect moment, look back at us over your shoulder as you walk down the aisle and know that we are right behind you.

The Day I Shot Cupid

Texting or Sexing

kay, so let's be honest, texting is fun! It's flirty and dangerous. You can be more forward if you're shy, more honest if you're scared, and it's faster if you're antisocial. And, like anything really cool, if you overuse it, it can be a nightmare. The first time a guy texts you, it's awesome! You can't wait to write back something witty and wait by your phone for a response. (**NOTE:** You are waiting. By the phone. For his response.)

And here it comes, the flirty text that will start it all. You've got his attention, it's hot, and you've found a rhythm! It's been an amazingly wordy week and a half. He hasn't called or taken you out, but he hasn't blown you off either. Maybe he just needs more time, or maybe he's *supposed* to take an hour and a half to respond to your last text. Or maybe he hasn't turned his whole life over to your little text affair and is having a day. Like a normal person. Sorry, the truth hurts. News flash, maybe he's texting you while he's with the girl *he is on a date with*. Or else, loving the fact that he can flirt wildly and not commit to anything more solid. Or maybe he's just too stupid to know that you won't stand for that forever. Or will you?

Come on, ladies, we've got to be smarter than this! Do we want textin' or sexin'? It's cool to rely on modern means to get things rolling, but if we don't stop the electronic lovin' before it's gone too far, they won't. Hey mister—text me all you want, but after three days I need a phone call and some face-to-face lovin' to ensure what you really want is me and not a cyber-Sally, hassle-free, texting girlfriend. Can you say passive-aggressive, boys? I mean, what's next? Text sex?! I'll tell you what—it's already happening! Ew!

The Day I Shot Cupid

HIS TEXT

If you're a good girl . . .
I'll text you my penis size.

HER TEXT

Well big daddy . . . my nipple
dimensions are on the way.

HIS TENTH TEXT

62

Instead of cuddling and looking
into your eyes . . . I'm going to
shut my phone off and text you
tomorrow.

And we wonder why the relationship isn't
working? Say no to text relationships. Take his
BlackBerry away, and see what he's really
made of.

Jennifer Love Hewitt

IM in. IM out.
I'm Still on His IM.

h . . . stressful day at the office so sweetly interrupted by the instant message (IM) man of your dreams. What a great little invention. He can say hello, send kisses and smileys, and mess up your train of thought anytime he feels like it. And you can do the same. It's so sweet and . . . so much like stalking when you think about it. If you're there, he knows. If you're gone, he knows. Every time you're there and don't answer . . . he knows. Maybe they should have temporary IM restraining orders. Think about it. You break up, he moves out, you say good-bye to his friends, cry, gain weight, cry, get a new life, lose weight, move on, forget about him, go to work, get on your computer, and like from the dead, it emerges. The one thing you didn't do. THE BLOCK. The IM block that allows you freedom from the occasional

HEY dot dot dot

WHAT'S UP dot dot dot

YOU SEEING ANYBODY dot dot dot

I KNOW YOU'RE THERE dot dot dot

We must think of everything, girls! Why should we be prisoners on our own computers? Stop reading this and block him before it's too late! Run to your computer, don't walk!

Jennifer Love Hewitt

Love is a fire. But whether it is going to warm your heart or burn down your house, you can never tell.

—Joan Crawford

Three Strikes
YOU'RE OUT

If dates were like baseball, the three strikes you're out rule would still apply. There are lots of variations on the theme, but the outcome is the same. On my one and only blind date, I experienced three in one night. He called me "baby" before we even pulled out of the driveway, gave me Altoids twenty minutes in for "our kiss at the end of the night," and then tried to get me to play a game with him at the arcade because "that's what couples do." The appearance of my knight in shining armor was not what had been written in my childhood diaries. He was wearing alligator loafers (hello, PETA?), slacks that were cut too high (maybe he was expecting a flood?), and a shiny silk shirt. Yeah, I was about to go out with the neighborhood slick guy, except he obviously was from a time period before I was born. (**SIDE NOTE:** The reason they call it a blind date is because if you could see them you wouldn't go!)

Let me show you how this works. You're in public and the guy starts to show anger or aggression toward you and others.

STRIKE ONE.

Later in the evening you realize that the "friend" who dressed him, taught him those manners, and told him it was okay for him to behave this way on a date is his EX who is also his ROOMMATE.

STRIKE TWO.

And then at the climax of the evening (the only one you will experience) you go to a karaoke bar, "because that makes up for the last two hours of your life you will never get back," and realize you are with a man who knows every word to the Discovery Channel song and is proud of it! For those of you who don't know the song, the lyrics are . . . "you and me baby

The Day I Shot Cupid

ain't nothin' but mammals, so let's do it like they do on the Discovery Channel."

STRIKE THREE, YOU'RE OUT!

Now, although these scenarios sound dramatic, trust me, the three strike rule works when applied. Look, if he strikes out three times in one night, you don't want to go to that game again, and the hot dog probably wasn't very good.

HERE ARE SOME MORE STRIKES TO LOOK OUT FOR

1. He is more than fifteen minutes late.

2. He is driving his mother's car.

3. His mother is driving.

. . . .

1. If he can't stop looking at your chest.

2. If he can't stop looking at the waitress's chest.

3. If he can't stop looking at every girl's chest.

. . . .

Jennifer Love Hewitt

1. If he starts talking about himself and can't stop.

2. If he starts talking at breakfast in the morning and you just sat down.

3. If he basically tries to eat your face when kissing you good night.

. . . .

1. If he keeps saying, "That's so dumb" when you're talking.

2. If he's been living in his ex-wife's house.

3. If he keeps calling you by another girl's name.

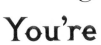

You're Out!!!

Something Smells

Okay, price of nice perfume—$50. Lotion and powder to go with it—$150. Victoria's Secret nightie—$45. Mascara, eyeliner, concealer, blush, gloss, and foundation—at least $250. And mani-pedi—at least $30. Just some of the things we do as women to get our guys all hot and bothered, and it works. It attacks them like the bird flu and makes them defenseless. We become sex goddesses, smelling of roses and vanilla, with smoky eyes and French tips, slinking across the room with our hair cascading around us, in a body-hugging nightie that we will never wear again.

And yet, romance (or that damn Cupid) shoves one more pin in our alluring balloon. A study was done a few years ago to find out what scent got men going. They were all blindfolded and asked to smell a bunch of different aromas. This is where you'll want to sit down. *Every one of them* picked the same thing. Was it exotic? Did it smell of unforgettable nights in Europe? Could it change your sex life forever? Not unless you find breakfast arousing. They all picked the smell of freshly baked cinnamon rolls. Are you kidding me?

Okay, my first two problems—who included breakfast in the perfume test? (Must have been a man.) And do I actually have to worry more about the factory girls from Pillsbury than their model exes? Honestly, what is the world coming to? I refuse to walk around with frosting behind my ears and cinnamon on my wrists. A French maid or a Playboy Playmate is okay to get your man's motor running, but to pretend to be a croissant? That is where dignity is lost. So save all of your beauty money, and I guess if you want to take him to bed, take him to breakfast.

The Day I Shot Cupid

Déjà Wardrobe

Okay, so we have all done it. Taken the walk. We have connected with someone, or some tequila bottle, and found ourselves in day two of the same outfit. Taken what is affectionately called THE WALK OF SHAME. **QUESTION:** How come John Travolta walks down the street with a theme song after dancing all night and everyone thinks he's cool? Yet we all can't get a cab or friendly "good morning" without judgment and misunderstanding. SO WHAT? I DIDN'T GO HOME! The outfit looked great last night, maybe it will look even better in the light of day. "He said he could see into my soul" (okay, maybe that's not a good reason to take the walk). Sometimes stuff happens! What are we supposed to do? Turn our car into a mini walk-in so that others approve? Not ever follow our hearts down Impulsive Street? And why do we care? And here's a bone—who made it the walk of shame? Why can't it be the "I had a good time walk" or "the walk of accomplishment"? Maybe we just all care too much about what others think.

So right here, right now, let's change it! NO MORE SHAME! Take a walk whatever time you want, with a theme song or without, but hold your head high. It's time to be proud of our decisions, and remember, the outfit you wear tonight, you better like in the morning.

The Day I Shot Cupid

When Your Relationship Comes to a

Skid....Mark

This is not for those with delicate stomachs, so beware. In relationships there are lots of big moments, cliffhangers, and showstoppers, and then what I like to call "oh no he didn'ts!" Let me set the scene: it's another beautiful day in your dreamy relationship with Mr. Perfect and you decide to be a domestic goddess for your man. Besides writing "Mrs._____" over and over again on a piece of paper, the other way to pretend you're in domestic bliss is to do his laundry, see your whites next to his whites, your thongs next to his briefs. It's the moment

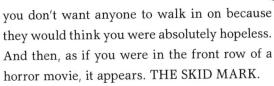

you don't want anyone to walk in on because they would think you were absolutely hopeless. And then, as if you were in the front row of a horror movie, it appears. THE SKID MARK.

Stop everything. Unless you have had bad fish or the twenty-four-hour flu, there is just no excuse. WIPE HARDER! And if you know there's a chance that something might get left behind, wash them yourself, or burn them. I have been introduced to Mr. Brown and I didn't handle it well at first. I screamed and ran to the opposite end of the house. Why? I

The Day I Shot Cupid

don't know. Maybe I thought it would leave or clean itself or I was just dreaming. Then, with the *Rocky* theme song in my head, I decided that no brown ugly was going to get me down. So back I went! I grabbed those undies, with tongs of course, and threw them in the machine. I felt like a real woman. I knew that oodles of women had washed skids before me. I felt domestic and ready to take on whatever the world had to offer. I wondered if I would look at him differently, pay closer attention to what he was eating, and wonder every time if I would come face-to-face with it again. By the way, after that, he did the laundry.

Jennifer Love Hewitt

Natural Dilemma

So you're out with your guy, and it is breakfast time at your favorite café. The sun is shining, your skin glows perfect in the light, his eyes are still a little bit puffy from waking up, his bed-head is irresistible, and your guy can't stop staring at you. The type of staring you hope other women see because (a) you want witnesses and (b) you know for a brief moment of time they will be jealous and wish they were with him. Oh, but he is so not with them! He is yours and so happy to be a slave to the sparkle in your eyes! (P.S. Sparkle is provided by hot boyfriend staring.) And then it happens. And, oh ladies, it has happened to all of us. The moment that he says, "YOU ARE THE MOST

BEAUTIFUL WOMAN IN THE WORLD. I LOVE IT WHEN YOU DON'T WEAR MAKE-UP. I WANT TO BE WITH THE GIRL IN SWEATS AND NO MAKEUP FOREVER."

You are floored for many reasons. First, you have to forget the $30 you spent on hottie products, but, more important, all of that worry you've had for years, thinking of how you could erase supermodels so you could be noticed. Getting up two hours earlier than him to put on makeup so he doesn't see you without the mask. Worried that guy 187 didn't call because he met someone prettier. It's gone. Vanished. It only took one guy, your guy, to make you feel more beautiful than you could have imagined. Forget burning bras, you want to burn it all! Every product. And feel free in your naked beauty. So you kiss him, a big one that says I'll thank you now and later. You sit back and feel like the queen you are. You look around at the other women and wonder if they've had such a moment and, if not, hope they do. You are the natural Heidi Klum walk-

Jennifer Love Hewitt

ing down the runway of no-worries and everyone wants what you're selling. (Cue the record scratch.) WHAT THE HELL WAS THAT?! Did your guy just check out another girl? And not just with his eyes, but did he just turn his head? And for the girl in the March *Vogue* cover outfit and full makeup? And is he really trying to play it off like I didn't see it?

And why did that skank buzz-kill my moment?! This has happened to all of us. To me, way too many times. And I personally will never get it. **QUICK QUESTION, GUYS:** If you love us, your partner, with no makeup, but your head turns toward the girl who has spent four hours in the bathroom, what are we supposed to do? And the excuses kill me. One guy said, and I quote, "Baby, I wasn't looking at that girl, my neck hurt and I was stretching it out." Guy two said, "Girl? What girl? I thought that was a dude." And, my personal favorite, from guy number three: "You know, a lot of people have noticed it is hard for me to focus on one thing, maybe I have adult ADD."

The Day I Shot Cupid

Seriously, they will go to any length to protect the right to stare. To admire someone's beauty is natural, but the head-turning, dead-mouth drooling, and saying that you love us natural and then gawking at America's Next Top Model is really hard to swallow. So what does it all mean? They should all be killed, that's what it means (said like the little kid in *The Shining*—sorry, that was my inside voice talking!). Should we express the way it makes us feel? Or do we, and this sounds easy, accept it as a thing that men do that's harmless, and unless they leave you at the café to follow the skirt home, don't worry. Be annoyed, but don't worry. MEN WILL ALWAYS LOOK.

So next time it happens, brush it off. And no matter what your inner voice tells you, know that if he left you it would be his biggest mistake. For the extremely insecure, the category I sometimes fall into, never let his wandering eye make you feel like you are not good enough. It's like a dog that is full and fat. It doesn't need food or want food, but if it's there it will beg for

Jennifer Love Hewitt

it. And remember, it's in our nature to want what we can't have. On the other hand, even if guys have to stare, it's a part of their nature, blah, blah, blah, but it's not okay if it hurts you. If it bothers you, that's one thing. If it hurts you, talk to him. And to the guys who might be reading this, be gentle. Looking at other girls while we are standing there can hurt. And then maybe some of you should be happy with the woman you have. In a relationship, don't look backward or forward, look right next to you. You are probably luckier than you realize. I say this to everyone. Love and relationships are already complicated, and making your partner feel like you'd rather be somewhere else doesn't help anything. There are a lot of people in the world to be with, and there will always be someone smarter, prettier, or more interesting.

If girls are putting it out there, guys are going to pick it up. They are not in a relationship with you and actively looking for something else. They are just doing what my boyfriend and I call "the register." They are registering

The Day I Shot Cupid

the opposite sex as a slight release of the old single guy and their right as "your guy" to still be able to look without it destroying you. It doesn't mean they want to run off and start a life with every girl they look at (that's in *our* heads). It's strictly physical and not emotional. By the way, we as women should register, too! Ladies, try to accept guys for who they are and don't take it personally. Guys, be more sensitive to your partner, and if you have to look, FOR THE LOVE OF GOD, WEAR SUNGLASSES!

OKAY—

the book has officially been hijacked by a MAN, who is funny, I trust, and has insight into the female mind. I hope you find what you read next as enlightening and inspiring as I did. True to women's form, I had to jump in every now and then!

BuTTinski,
or Does My
Butt Look Big?

(men hope so...)

"I like big butts and I cannot lie." Boy, Sir Mix-a-lot was a genius. No truer words have ever been spoken. The rear end or the booty has been the subject of fascination for the male species since the Stone Age.

I'm here to tell you, as a man, a guy, or whatever you want to call me, what we REALLY like. We like your BUTT, and we like it BIG. ♥ ♥ ♥ *Hold on a second! JLH here! I have to jump in! Did a man just say he likes our butts? And big? Then what has the last ten years of self-*

torture been about? Why didn't we know this be-fore and where is the nearest Baskin-Robbins? Sorry, continue. ♥ ♥ ♥ It's the last impression guys have of you when you're walking away. It's like the end credits of a movie. It's what we envision as something we can grab and hold. Something that will keep us warm and protect us from tropical storms because we can hide un-der it. But somehow in the last thirty years some-one thought the butt should be smaller, tiny, like an eight-year-old boy's even. WHAT!@#$%%? (NEEDLE SCRATCH.)

Ladies, ladies, ladies, let me tell you some-thing. Stop trippin' on yo' butt. Let your man decide how big it should be for you. ♥ ♥ ♥ *JLH again! Okay, he can decide how big, but I have to carry it in my pants. You want a bigger butt? Say the word. Whatever you want, sweetheart. Sorry, keep going.* ♥ ♥ ♥ If you look at the history of film, from Olivia de Havilland in the beginning, all the way through the sixties, seventies (espe-cially Russ Meyer films), Kelly LeBrock in the eighties and the nineties with J.Lo and Salma

The Day I Shot Cupid

Hayek, etc., women have always had big, round, beautiful derrieres. You notice how I didn't mention Cate Blanchett and Nicole Kidman in that sentence. Classy, beautiful women, nonetheless, but no junko in the trunko. (Although, I will say, as far as Englishwomen go, Kate Winslet does have a nice badonkadonk.)

We men worship your heinie. First of all, *more cushin' for pushin', more round to ground,* and *bootylicious,* are all terms that apply to women that men love. ♥ ♥ ♥ *Oh, you know who it is! If I could just eat a double-double right now and shake it naked, I would. This is hot! Women everywhere—pay attention. A man who knows other men, and is surrounded by a city of beautiful, thin women, wants you bootylicious. Come on, tell me this is not the best day ever!* ♥ ♥ ♥ Shapely and curvy is what turns men on, not NOSITOL (no ass at all). It says that our women are sexy, strong, and yummy. When we see a woman with the kitchen sink as her backside, we just want to kiss you all over after we tackle you like a fullback on the thirty-yard line at Soldier Field.

Jennifer Love Hewitt

I feel that women somehow (maybe when aerobics started . . . damn you, JANE FONDA!!!) have lost touch with what men desire and are trying to go against the natural grain of BONERISM.

Let me tell you something, MEN DON'T WANT OLIVE OYL! They want *Attack of the 50 Ft. Woman.* It goes back to our genetics, girls. Google it. I hate to see ladies always worried and saying, "Do these pants make my butt look big?" God, I hope so. ♥ ♥ ♥ *Yep, you guessed it, JLH again. I just have to say—what?? God, I love this man! And where has this secret colony of butt-lovers been living? We don't* want *to ask if our butts look big. But we thought anything over a size 0, which isn't even a size anyway, was a no-no. Again, sorry for interrupting, tell us more!* ♥ ♥ ♥ Men don't want sticks. I'm serious, girls. We like juicy and firm, or juicy and jiggly. Have you ever heard a man say, "HEY LOOK AT THAT ASS! IT'S SO FLAT. COOL, LET ME GET SOME OF THAT!!!!"?

NOOOOO. Stop reading magazines, ladies. It ain't reality. Those are starved bitches who

The Day I Shot Cupid

survive on Starbucks, cigarettes, and Valtrex, and most are fourteen years old. ♥ ♥ ♥ *JLH is SO glad you just said that! As women, if we said this we would get slapped. And P.S., have you ever seen a super-skinny girl with a smile on her face? No, she's too hungry.* ♥ ♥ ♥ Being neurotic about your backside is not sexy to men. Sexy, to men, is owning your rump roast and daring your man to try and conquer it. Sexy, to men, is your attitude, and the attitude is in your eyes—when you look at us, and we see that stare you give and you're confident in who you are. That's what gets us going, because we think, "Dayyum, that chick knows what she wants. I hope she picks me." Hell, *voluptuous* has become a curse word to a lot of women. THAT'S WHAT MEN WANT!!

Here's an example: Have you ever seen a woman who's kinda big? She's got big boobs, a big butt, and thick legs. She wears heels and pants a little too tight. I know girls look at her and say, "WHO does she think SHE is with all that extra luggage? She better put THAT away."

Well, ladies, let me tell you, men look at her and say, "Woooo! I wanna tackle that lion. I wanna tame that beast!" You know you've seen women like this, and you might be one. Those women should be adored because they are confident in their size, and men love confidence. ♥ ♥ ♥ *Me again! I have to say this whole thing is shocking and great. I might actually be able to feel good about myself in a pair of skinny jeans eating a pint of ice cream. God bless you, Jamie Kennedy.* ♥ ♥ ♥ If you own who you are, then men will wanna own it with you. Enjoy yourself, and men will enjoy you also.

Which leads me to another thought—women can be so hard on other women. You're a sisterhood. Have each other's backs. ♥ ♥ ♥ *Sorry to keep butting in—no pun intended—but you're right, we are a sisterhood, except some girls didn't get the memo and are mean, which makes us defensive and judgmental. But hey, I'm so happy about the big butt thing, I'll look at being nicer to other girls.* ♥ ♥ ♥ It's true. Women judge each other so hard. They'll look a woman up and

89

The Day I Shot Cupid

down and say, "Look at her, she got her lips done, she got her cheeks done, she got her nose done. Hell! That's not even her real head!"

I personally think women get boob implants to compete with other women, and men get hair transplants to compete with other men. It's not for the opposite sex. I mean, we'll take fake boobs if you've got them, but we'd rather take what God gave you, small or big. As long as you're cool with it, we're cool with it, and if you want a little procedure because it will make you feel better about yourself, go for it. Grab that scalpel. We all do a little nip and tuck now and then (God knows these aren't my real pecs). But it saddens me to see women be so hard on themselves about the body they think they have, as opposed to the body that men are dying to get all over. We love your big hips, your big butt (more to spoon with), your big boobs (more to keep us warm), and your little tummy pooch, that's where we wanna crawl in and live. We know it's safe there. ♥ ♥ ♥ *JLH . . . See, girls, there are good ones out there!* ♥ ♥ ♥ Just my two cents.

—Jamie Kennedy

Find a guy who calls you beautiful instead of hot, who calls you back when you hang up on him, who will lie under the stars and listen to your heartbeat, or will stay awake just to watch you sleep. . . . Wait for the boy who kisses your forehead, who wants to show you off to the world when you are in sweats, who holds your hand in front of his friends, who thinks you're just as pretty without makeup on. One who is constantly reminding you of how much he cares and how lucky he is to have YOU . . . the one who turns to his friends and says, that's her.

—Unknown

His and Her Thrones

The bathroom. The friend that knows all your secrets, maybe too many. The sacred place where we get ready for the world. The magic passageway that we step through for a big date. We go in a potential hottie and come out a showstopper. It's where a guy goes from a boy to a man, with cologne and a crisp white button-down. It's more than a bathroom, it's your sanctuary. And then someone invented his and her sinks. What were they thinking? Hello reality, good-bye mystery. I'm all for domesticity and sharing space, but not *that space*. I didn't always feel this way. I thought it would be the ultimate in romance, until I realized it's not just *men* who need a little mystery.

Let's be honest, it's not hot to see a man clip his nose hairs, rub his butt, clean out his ears, or worse, discover he doesn't do any of those things! And men definitely don't want to see us shave our underarms, pluck our eyebrows, lather on anticellulite cream, Nair our nifty mustache, and struggle with figure-smoothing shorts (*P.S., I love those shorts!*). We want to picture our guy in a hot shower with water dripping from his biceps, his white teeth sparkling in the mirror (like Edward from *Twilight*), barely containing his excitement to see us. Now, that is hot! And guys want to picture us in tiny black lace panties, high heels, with our hair half up, half down, and a little in our face, dancing to "Let's Get It On," putting perfume in all the right places and slipping slowly into our little black dress à la Audrey Hepburn. So I say sharing some things is good, just not everything. Let mystery be your secret weapon of

The Day I Shot Cupid

romance. Let him have his fantasy of you and you in return cherish your alone time in the magic chamber that is the bathroom. Trust me, no man will be offended by these separate quarters. In fact, you might even be the woman of his dreams.

Jennifer Love Hewitt

WWW.ZIPIT.COM

*H*ave you ever had words fly out of your mouth like a bad meal? I suffer from this on a daily basis. I need someone to invent a mouth zipper. SPEAKING OF ZIPPERS, don't you just despise the men and women with no moral values or self-control and with downright slutty behavior who can't keep their zippers closed—oops, see what I'm talking about . . . no self-control! SPEAKING OF CONTROL, don't you wish you could turn your back for five seconds without some pea-brain bimbo trying to make the love of your life an afternoon snack—oops . . . I did it again! Inventors, please listen to my plea: MOUTH ZIPPER. While I'm on this subject, here is a novel idea. Let people be in love. If you see two people happy, keep your mitts to yourself.

Just know these destroyers of happiness will never penetrate the inner lining of the heart we occupy. I'll tell you why these people are out there; it's to show us who we can trust. There will always be sluts and man-whores, but there will also be good women and even better men who won't stray from their hearts' desire because something new has been added to the menu. It is our job to send those lost yet slutty souls our light and sympathy, because at the end of the day it must be so sad to love yourself so little that you'd be willing to become the joke, the cocktail-hour topic, or, worst of all, the reason someone else will find it difficult to love and trust again. Guess I couldn't zip it on that one.

Jennifer Love Hewitt

Let's Play "We"

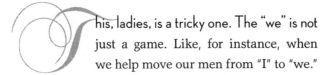his, ladies, is a tricky one. The "we" is not just a game. Like, for instance, when we help move our men from "I" to "we."

HIM: "I'm going to dinner at 8 p.m."

US: "No, actually, *we* are going to dinner."

HIM: "*I* just came back from vacation in Mexico."

US: "No, actually, *we* just came back from vacation in Mexico."

I don't believe for a minute that this is a mantactic, a reason not to commit. I think it's complete unawareness of the joint relationship effort. They are used to traveling alone, whereas women tend to travel in groups. For instance *we*, from the time we are little, go to the bathroom together. *They* go it alone. *They* take their computers and go to Starbucks. *We* go with the girls for drinks. *They* go backpacking in Europe. *We* go for all-girls spa weekends. *They* like to play alone (you know what I mean). *We* prefer not to play alone (you also know what I mean). We can't be hard on men about this one. We have to help them. When they say "I," help them say "we." If you and your guy are with other people and he says, "*I* ate at the best restaurant last night," just simply follow it up with "Yeah, *we* had the best food!" It will eventually change his thinking.

And men, relax, just because we want you to include us in the moment with the powerful "we" doesn't mean marriage. Women don't think "we" is the house, the dog, the joint bank account, the wedding, the babies, and the end (well, maybe some do, but we don't claim those girls). For women, it's just a small, considerate step toward really respecting us. It's including us in your life and showing no fear in sharing your existence. It's important for both sexes to keep their identities, but it's also sometimes important to share. We were all taught that in, what, first grade, I think. Just try to be more aware, guys, and help them out, ladies. Trust me, "we" will all be happier.

Breaking Up
Is Easy
to Do;

Surviving

It Is the
Hard Part

(Can't Live With 'Em, Can't Live
Without 'Em, Can't Shoot 'Em!
Well, Maybe in Some States.)

Falling in love is awfully simple,
but falling out of love is simply awful.

—Anonymous

Put Your
Big-Girl Pants On
and Get Over It

reakups, good-byes, endings, however you see it, are hard. It feels like someone is driving over you with his car. You don't know how you will ever get out of bed, eat again, or stop eating. You keep crying and telling the story, and beating yourself up for not seeing it sooner or doing it better. He goes from being the love of your life to your ex-boyfriend to a jerk to a piece of bleep to just a bleeping bleep. The radio stations only play love songs to torture you. Romantic comedies are on every channel. And only really happy couples eat at restaurants, go grocery shopping, and now, for some strange reason, stop and smile at you. You start to notice kittens because soon you will live alone with ninety cats and one fern. All the fruit you crave comes in bunches or pairs—even fruit hates you! The one time you do eat out, the guy and girl next to you get engaged and ask you to take their first photo (this actually happened to me the day after I had to end my engagement—cue the crocodile tears). Your eyes are so swollen shut from crying it's impossible to see your future. Even old people and babies, who you can never get mad at, now seem like horrible people because babies have felt no pain and know not of your suffering, and old people don't have to worry about finding someone new. And then one day, when everyone has let you live in misery for the needed amount of drama, it has to end. Like a cavalcade of angels with maxi-pad wings come your girlfriends. And these words change it all: "PUT YOUR BIG-GIRL PANTS ON AND GET OVER IT!"

The Day I Shot Cupid

And you do. (a) You've eaten so much you have only big-girl pants, and (b) Being depressed is not productive. Even if you have to pretend to be happy for a while, your spirit will follow. Remember, it always gets worse before it gets better. And when it gets better, it gets great. I've just gone through it and I've come out on the other side. I have a new respect for myself. I have been able to look inside and figure out who I truly am. I know that I am the marriage type and can be in a committed relationship, even if he was not the right one. And I know now that I truly can survive anything. Sometimes it's in the toughest moments that you learn the most about yourself, and the more you know yourself, the less you are willing to give away.

Jennifer Love Hewitt

It Was

Vagazzaling

So there I was, trying to heal from my trampled heart. Trying to think of anything I could do to get out of this funk. I learned to crochet finger puppets, because any guy I date next will have that as a requirement, right? I perfected my "I'm over him and movin' on" voice. My ultimate discovery came when I realized that if you stare at the ceiling and start counting around 11:30 p.m., you will reach 1,486 by 4 a.m. I am so glad I learned that. A lot like algebra—not! And then somewhere between the late show and the early show, it hit me. The lightbulb I had been waiting for, THE BEST IDEA I'VE EVER HAD. I need a spray tan!!!!!!!!!!!!

God, I need to get a life. Spray tans seem very exciting after 1,500 conversations with your dog. It's time to let someone in my house, and bring with them a little color. That's right, soon I would be a walking caramel macchiato. Angelique was the magic woman's name. She would be the first person I talked to in weeks and the one to start the cocoa-colored make-over. When she arrived, I was so excited to start my transformation, and then color layer by color layer my confidence grew.

She told me about this new beauty trend. It would not only change my outer appearance, but how I felt about myself on the inside. She said it would add a little sparkle to my life. I called it "VAGAZZALING." She wanted to put Swarovski crystals on my hoo-ha. The lack of traffic on my hoo-ha highway at that moment and my fear of lying sober and naked while a woman puts crystals on my little lady made me hesitate. Then I wondered why. In my head

Jennifer Love Hewitt

I couldn't have a "vagazzled" area without someone to see it, but I was wrong. I should do it for me. It should look like my favorite denim jacket from the eighties and be just for my viewing pleasure. So I lay down. It was very fast and not awkward at all. And what I saw when the mirror and I met was amazing. The once pale, sad girl who couldn't figure out how to move on from her breakup had transformed into a bronzed sex goddess with the prettiest hoo-ha in my neighborhood.

For the next week I had this uncontrollable urge to show everyone my crystal delight. Thank God I fought that and kept the adoration society to one. It's true; I had started a love affair with my lower region disco ball and before I knew it, I felt great again. So if you find yourself down and out, or just want to have a sparkly secret in your pants—go for it! Boost your confidence and get out of the dumps any way you can. But don't bedazzle it, VAGAZZLE it!!

The Day I Shot Cupid

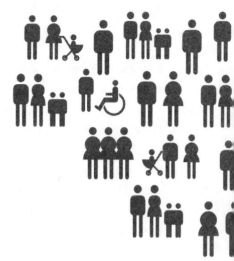

Table for One

 Well, here I am, eating alone. Not to sound needy, but I've never done this before. Never ordered without someone to discuss it with. Never had the waiter say, "Just you? [Weird feeling-sorry-for-me pause and then] This way, ma'am." Why am I a *ma'am*? Is it because I'm alone? As I sit in a pretty empty restaurant, I notice that everyone here is alone. Have these sweet

patrons come out to support me in my table for one? Is this restaurant *called* Table for One? Or is it just that I find myself in a business stopover hotel where most people are actually alone? It's sweet and sad in a way, to watch them all not want to be by themselves so badly that everyone is on the phone. Even me. I can't call enough people to fill in the space between "More water, ma'am?" and my entrée.

So why is it that we can't be alone? What's wrong with laughing to yourself about the funny thing that happened that day? Saying in a hushed tone, "Wow, this tastes good!" Maybe it's because when you can tell someone a funny story, it also makes their day, and a laugh that is shared is food for your soul. And maybe sharing something that tastes good between two people who care enough about each other to share a meal is the stuff life is made of. A few brief conversations with myself, two margaritas, and a really nice meal later, I decided it would be a very long time before I ask for a moment alone again.

The Day I Shot Cupid

In Whom Can We Trust

Have you ever really looked at the word *trust*? I mean, we've all talked about it, had it, not had it, given it and been sorry, or wanted to be able to give it so badly, but have been so haunted by the ghosts of the past that we couldn't. But have we really looked at it? I did today, for the first time. I wrote it down on a piece of paper and studied it like the Da Vinci code, and there it was, right there in the middle of this simple five-letter word. The answer we all seek, but can't or don't want to see, in the middle of the word *trust* is the word *us*. Yeah, makes blaming your issues on someone else kind of difficult.

Maybe finding trust is so hard because it's not about looking at another person. Maybe it's about looking at ourselves. When things get tough and scary, can you be trusted not to run? When you feel insecure or threatened and have had your trust tested and it failed, will you be able to trust or will you live in fear of being hurt again? Can you be trusted to live by the same rules you ask others to live by? Can you be trusted with someone's heart? It suddenly all becomes clearer. First we have to trust ourselves. And if we can be trusted (with someone's heart), if we can trust (another person), and, most important, trust (in ourselves), then we will always be okay.

Really finding the ability to trust is the hardest thing to do. I'm still working on this one. Because when it's broken, it feels like something inside you dies. But someone is worth all you have to give. Take a long look at yourself. Trust yourself and then trust others. Everything will be okay . . . trust me.

The Day I Shot Cupid

Love means to commit oneself without guarantee, to give oneself completely in the hope that our love will produce love in the loved person. Love is an act of faith, and whoever is of little faith is also of little love.

—Unknown

You Love Me,
You Really
Love Me . . .

or Maybe Not

don't know about you, but I'm pretty strong. Not a lot gets me down or damages my spirit. But I do find a difference between my inner and outer self. If someone attacks my brain, body, or image, I am fine. Sure, it sucks, but from the core of who I am comes this way of not letting it get to me. I am affected by it and then I move on. But when it comes to my heart, a bad or unkind review on my ability to love leaves me crippled. Someone attacking my heart is like being shot. I lose all ability to be strong. And here comes the really messed-up part, and I know it's not just me—people can say nice things all day long and I'll miss them or brush them off, but the one bad thing feels like it's being shouted through a megaphone pressed directly against my eardrum! So why do we always believe the worst reviews?

I think it's because to truly love or be in your highest self makes us very vulnerable. I also think it's really simple. We all care what others think of us, don't try to pretend you don't, because I know you do. And if someone doesn't like our outside we can take it as opinion or taste, but if someone doesn't like our inside, it's an attack on who we are. But here is the upside—we all get through it and most of the time we get stronger. The downside, however, can be devastating. If we wear our worst reviews like a backpack, they travel with us. The only way to beat the bad review is to leave

Jennifer Love Hewitt

it behind. Please don't take it with you, it's not healthy. And NEVER change who you are because of a bad review. Remember what they say: opinions are like . . . well, you know . . . and everybody's got one! And let's be honest, most critics are insecure and not happy with who they are either.

Please know that slight nitpicking and teasing in any relationship is healthy, but breaking someone's spirit is never okay. A bad love review does not mean you are a horrible person, it means you may not be right for them, and why would you want to be with someone who feels that way? It's okay to ask more of someone or to be loved differently, but it's never okay to damage someone's heart. The "love slayers," as we will now call them, learn of their destruction only by seeing it at work.

So here's what I will ask of you—next time you meet one of those love slayers in the dark alleys of relationships, be strong, take the review, look him or her in the face, and say, "Thank you, I will try and work on that for the

The Day I Shot Cupid

next person." Tell him or her that you feel this situation isn't right for you anymore and walk away. In two seconds you have stepped on the slayers' review, been stronger than they ever thought you could be, and fought off the bad-review arrow headed straight for your heart. Some people think it's the first impression that matters most, but I think it's the last.

Jennifer Love Hewitt

Get Moving!

orking out with a regular trainer has saved my life. Having a friend, female companion, and motivator has proven to be my best decision yet, especially in matters of my heart. Yep, that love thing again. Working out really helped me through it. Stevie, my fabulous trainer, was kind enough to share her secrets with all of you. So start the healing process and let the makeover begin!

—JLH

There are generally three ways to go after your heart has been run over: (a) down Ben & Jerry's Lane, (b) Alanis Morissette's *Jagged Little Pill*, aka the "get back/female empowering anthem route," or (c) the least popular, last house on the left, "take good care of yourself, honor your loss, and forge a foundation of self-esteem." What on earth am I talking about here? You've got to move AND you've got to sweat! Even if it's just for twenty minutes a day. I vote for motion vs. no motion. Every little thing you do for yourself counts. You count. I try to use these unhappy but inevitable "opportunities" to fine-tune myself from the inside out, so that I may emerge from these situations stronger, more together, and healthier.

Love always teases me about my affection for Einstein, boring medical journals, and other areas of science geekery, but check this out. Low endorphin and serotonin levels make us reach for calorie-dense, sugary, fat-rich foods. Endorphins and serotonin are hormones that our body naturally manufactures. When the levels of these hormones are too low, besides the over-whelming food cravings that occur, we get stressed, anxious, and irritable. When we have enough of these hormones, we feel calm, confident, and balanced. It's really no wonder that we reach for the comfort foods we do during emotionally charged times. We seek to regulate our moods. These sugars and fats give us those same feelings of ease, satisfaction, or anesthesia that those hormones do, EXCEPT they begin a constant cycle where we crave them, seeking out those initial feelings of comfort. So really, comfort foods aren't so comforting in this format.

So, without breaking out my pointer with the little black tip from grade school, the BEST way I know to get these natural chemicals flowing, for us to feel better all around and put our hearts back in our chests where they belong, is to get moving!! Exercise and exorcise!!

Find a friend. Find a buddy (dog or cat). Find the time!

Things are easier with an accomplice—I mean good friend. I got through a world-class

121

awful breakup with the help of my pals Wendell Hooper and Chris Zwirner. We got ourselves some running shoes (get some appropriate workout shoes), signed up for FUN group fitness classes at our local gym (go find something physical AND interesting in a group format), and took to our local parks (again, get out of the house!).

We didn't care how far we went or how fast we ran or what we looked like doing it. That doesn't matter. We laughed, we moved, we cried sometimes, and then started to feel better! I STARTED TO FEEL BETTER. Moving around starts a beautiful but slow upward spiral of positive effects. Not to say I didn't still get moments of sadness, frustration, and, the less pleasant to admit, anger. But the times I did feel them got fewer and my self-esteem grew stronger. Admittedly, my legs and booty weren't looking too shabby either! Nothing says "revenge" better than looking and feeling healthy and beautiful (not that I condone harboring such feelings, but it DOES feel good

Jennifer Love Hewitt

when you run into your ex and you look really happy and healthy from the inside out!).

THE BUDDY: Numerous studies (here I go again) have indicated that petting your dog or cat reduces stress and lowers your blood pressure. It's true! The interactive touching is nurturing and soothing. It's essential that we maintain a feeling of intimacy with another living thing while we are mending our hearts. If you don't have a buddy or aren't able to in your place, seek out your local rescue or animal shelters and volunteer to walk or care for the animals there. You would be surprised what even as little as a few hours a week will do for you, not to mention how happy the animal you are comforting would feel. Personally I feel compelled to mention that my dogs have seen me through two houses, one marriage, four births, three funerals, and a parade of irritating dating scenarios. As living things, we heal each other. Our health is the sum total of our minds, our bodies, and our spirits. This wonderful feeling of connectedness fills all three.

The Day I Shot Cupid

THE TIME: In short, make the time to move around. Take a crowbar to your schedule if you have to, but treat yourself like an honored and welcome guest. Make sure you put good energy back into your life. If you find yourself with possibly too much free time because your former partner isn't there anymore, it's doubly important to have something with equal physical and emotional value in its place. Too much free time leads to the refrigerator.

THE "WORKING IT OUT" WORKOUT: Here's my favorite workout, which will get you feeling and looking strong and beautiful. Do this three days a week, in the gym or at home.

What you'll need:

GOOD, LOUD MUSIC

A mat

A jump rope

A set of hand weights (5–10 pounds)

A dodge ball ($3.99 in the toy department), or wad up a bath towel

A chair (or a bench if you're at the gym)

A tiara! If Love can take bubble baths in one, we can work out in them as well. She's right—you actually do feel lovely wearing one!

NOTE: YES I DO THIS AND NO I'M NOT KIDDING AROUND!

This is a pretty thorough training session. It should take about an hour or so, depending on your speed. Once you get acclimated to the routine, you can really go through this efficiently. Go at a manageable pace. Take a short break when you need to. And smile—it opens up the doors to your heart.

 10-minute warm-up run on the treadmill or take it around the block!

*Part One—*UPPER BODY

10 Push-ups *(full-body or bent-knee position—you're still using 75 percent of your body weight if your knees are bent!)*

Grab a heavy set of hand weights for the next five exercises.

20 Chest Flies—*lying on your back*

20 Bench Presses—*lying on your back*

Jennifer Love Hewitt

20 Overhead Shoulder Presses—
sitting in a chair/on a bench

20 Biceps Curls—*standing up*

20 Triceps Kick Backs—*Bending at the
hip, so it looks like you're bowing to the
queen, lift your elbows so your upper arms
are parallel to the ground; gently "kick back"
the weight so your arms straighten out.
Repeat 19 more times!*

Keep your core engaged (tighten your tummy)
when performing these!

Jump rope for 1 minute *(This can be
really, really fun or frustrating. It may take
a minute to remember just how to jump rope,
but you WILL get it, I promise. Lighten up
and think like a kid! Once you've managed
this, you can jump rope for one- to three-
minute intervals at a time.)*

Do this block of exercises two or more times!!

Push-up position, please! Don't forget to jump rope after each set. It will help shake things out. ("Things" are what I refer to as tight muscles. It's in the same category as "thingamajiggy" and "whatziewhoozies.")

 ## FITNESS INTERMISSION

10-minute jog on treadmill or take it around the block again—say "hi" to neighbors this time.

· ·

*Part Two—*LOWER BODY

· ·

You may hold on to hand weights during these exercises to make it more challenging.

2O Right Leg Forward Lunges

2O Left Leg Forward Lunges

2O Standing Calf Raises
(Gotta look good in heels!)

Jennifer Love Hewitt

15 Basic Squats—*Think Sumo wrestler here; squat down just to the height of your knee, then stand back up again. Make sure your knees and feet are a little wider than shoulder distance apart.*

Jump rope for 1 minute.

1-minute Inner-Thigh Ball Squeezes—*Lying flat on your back, place the dodge ball between your knees. Gently squeeze the ball, using medium pressure. Your inner thighs will feel "spicy."*

1-minute Hamstring and Booty Lift-Ups—*Using the same position as above, hold the ball firmly with your knees and gently lift your pelvis all the way up and then lower it down to the ground. Lift your pelvis about 8 to 10 inches off the ground. You'll start to feel your hamstrings and booty get tight. Breathe. These are very effective.*

Repeat the lower-body section 2 more times.

The Day I Shot Cupid

FITNESS INTERMISSION

*10-minute light jog for the last time,
taking it around the block. Your legs
should feel heavy, but do it anyway—
they will loosen up.*

. . . .
Part Three—**CORE/BOOTY**
. . . .

Use a towel or your hands to support your
head.

20 Basic Crunches—*Keep your chin up
and gently lift your chest off the ground, about
4 inches up and back.*

20 2-Part Lift Crunches—*Lift high,
higher, and highest, then go back down all the
way. You're only lifting up about an inch and
a half each time.*

20 Bicycle Kicks—*Bring opposite knee
and elbow in to the chest (almost close enough
to touch) then switch. Go smoothly and*

Jennifer Love Hewitt

evenly. Make sure to extend the leg out when you're switching sides, so it looks like you are "pedaling." Count each of the kicks up to 20.

3 30-second Body Planks. *Lying flat on your mat, facing the ground, come up on your elbows and toes. Your elbows should line up below your shoulders. Your legs should be long, but not locked out. If this is too much weight to lift, bend your knees onto the mat. Again, this will be about 75 percent of your body weight. You can increase the intervals as you get stronger. This will strengthen your core and your back, and give you a light shoulder workout.*

And last, but oh so not least:

Clamshells!!!! Because really, jeans are expensive and it's important to keep this area looking good! *Lie on your side, in what I call the TV position. Rest your head on your hand. Bring both knees up to where your belly button is, stacking the feet. You will look like you were sitting in a chair that fell over. Place a light weight on your top knee and hold it there with your hand. Lift the top leg up and down. Make sure your foot also lifts up to the same height as your knee. (Just like a suitcase—one side doesn't raise higher than the other when opening.) Do this 50 times at a comfortable pace. Folks, it's going to smart . . . a lot. But this will shape up the booty in no time. Do the other side.*

CONGRATULATIONS, YOU'RE DONE!!!

Take a minute to turn off the music, sit down, close your eyes, and allow the body to "receive" what you've just done for it. Breathe in deeply through your nose, and then open your mouth to exhale (like you're fogging up a mirror), emptying out your lungs. Repeat, breathing deeply a few more times.

If this is the first time you're working out and getting physical, you'll be sore. Please

Jennifer Love Hewitt

stretch and continue with the training schedule. Not moving makes your muscles tighter. On that note, I highly suggest getting a massage every couple weeks. Your body is like a fine sports car; we have to make sure it gets tuned up, so it will keep performing well. I hope you experience as much joy and accomplishment as I have, being present and moving through the areas of my life.

Be well. Be happy. Be strong.

With love,
Stevie

The Day I Shot Cupid

Twenty Things to Do After a Breakup

1. Listen to *Jagged Little Pill* (Alanis Morissette).

2. Eat chocolate, but only for forty-eight hours.

3. Get out of bed, preferably within seventy-two hours.

4. Get out of the house (remember, your friends still have to know you, so shower).

5. Talk about something else.

6. Go to yoga.

7. Delete his number.

8. Change your number.

9. Make out with a stranger (he must be gorgeous or you'll feel worse).

10. Get a new outfit.

11. Get a new hairdo.

12. Call that guy you have always thought about.

13. Stop driving by his house (it's not *Fatal Attraction*).

14. Delete him from Facebook (refer to earlier IM chapter).

15. Don't have regrets.

The Day I Shot Cupid

16. Don't go to see romantic comedies.

17. Do something extreme
    (that you wouldn't normally do).

18. Don't go to the old "we" spots.

19. Take it one day at a time
    (we all have to take it one day at a time,
    that's how it works).

20. Know you won't die (you have to stick
    around so he can see what a mistake he
    made).

Jennifer Love Hewitt

The best and most beautiful things in the world cannot be seen or even touched. They must be felt with the heart.

—*Helen Keller*

Actual Facts About the Heart

Whenever we suffer a breakup, we can't help but wonder about the damage done to our hearts. Maybe some interesting facts about how truly strong the heart is will help us remember that the damage is just emotional:

♥ The average human heart, beating at seventy-two beats per minute, will beat approximately 2.5 billion times in a lifetime, which is about sixty-six years.

♥ It weighs on average 250g to 300g in females and 300g to 350g in males (for once, it's not women who have the weight problem).

♥ The human heart begins beating at a rate near the mother's, about seventy-five to eighty beats per minute, around twenty-one days after conception.

♥ There is no difference between male and female heartbeats before birth; it is only after birth and during full function as a male or female that they become different (boy, *how* different).

♥ The heart is the most critical organ of the human body, as it pumps oxygenated blood to feed the body's biological functions. Therefore, it is the part of the body you should take care of the most.

♥ High blood pressure and stress (breakups and fighting) can increase

The Day I Shot Cupid

the risk of developing heart disease. Of course, one must also consider other factors, such as lifestyle and overall health (mental and social as well as physical).

♥ The heart is essentially a muscle only a little larger than the fist (great things come in small packages).

Jennifer Love Hewitt

Let's Snuggle!
The Hormone That
Makes Us Do So

Oxytocin is the hormone that will be your new best friend. It is produced in both males and females. Oxytocin plays a role in response to maternal, sexual, and social behaviors. Even virgin female rats injected with oxytocin fawn and nuzzle anything nearby, protecting them as if they were their own. Studies show that oxytocin in females as well as in males is key to pair bonding. Oxytocin has been proven to increase trust and reduce fear (wonder if I can get it in a pill!). Our oxytocin levels rise when we are touched anywhere on our bodies, producing that "warm and fuzzy feeling." If there is a key that can help unlock the heart to love, it is oxytocin. Don't skip over the feeling when it happens—breathe it in and enjoy it. Oxytocin cocktail, anyone?

Jennifer Love Hewitt

In the Name of Love

kay, I know we have all been through this one. After you've stopped dating someone, everyone in your life has to tell you how awful he was. "Did you know he was cheating on you the whole time?" "Did you know that he hit on me at my birthday party?" "The first time I saw him, I knew he was all wrong for you." "He SO was not even cute!" You get the point. The initial purpose is sweet. It's to boost you up, make you feel special and like you were

too good for him anyway. But the internal con-
flict that you are experiencing is invisible to
those around you. You start to think, Why?
Why didn't anyone tell me I was with Satan?
Why didn't anyone tell me as my life was
dwindling away? And then you think, and why
tell me now? As if I need more bad news on top
off all the pain I'm feeling. Then you feel stupid for not seeing it. And it's only then that you
realize, sometimes the best good-bye is a nice
one. Leaving yourself with a good memory
will get you a lot further in the healing process.

Look, if it was good, you would still be in it.
It wasn't, so you're not. But wouldn't you rather
know that you were in it at one point for a reason? Of course you would. You want to know that
you chose the right person to spend time with
for that part of your life, that he was a good
person, and that, at that time, you made the
right choice. That your time together mattered
and you can take what you've learned here to
your next relationship. You want to remember

Jennifer Love Hewitt

good times, because it's only good that can fill up your heart so you can move on. Hatred makes you stagnant—it leaves no room for growth and isn't real.

I have apologized to friends and loved ones, but you can't say who I chose was wrong. That's for me to decide. Loving someone, even someone who you don't love anymore, for what they brought to your life, is you being your highest self. So, earmuffs. Let people know that your relationships are not to be gossiped about, that you love their support, but to support you with positive things, not negative. There are so many things to talk about, let's leave each other out of it.

The Day I Shot Cupid

An act of love that fails is just as
much a part of the divine life as
an act of love that succeeds,
for love is measured by fullness,
not by reception.

—*Harold Lokes*

This is the section where we truly bond. This is where there is no judgment, just support. I've had personal experience with how tough people's opinions can be; it's not fun, it can hurt. But we can also laugh and move on. Read ahead and know that I, too, have been there and will be there. Being a woman is the best thing in the world. It also comes with some tough times, hormones, and body changes, and while men grow old gracefully, we gracefully try not to grow old.

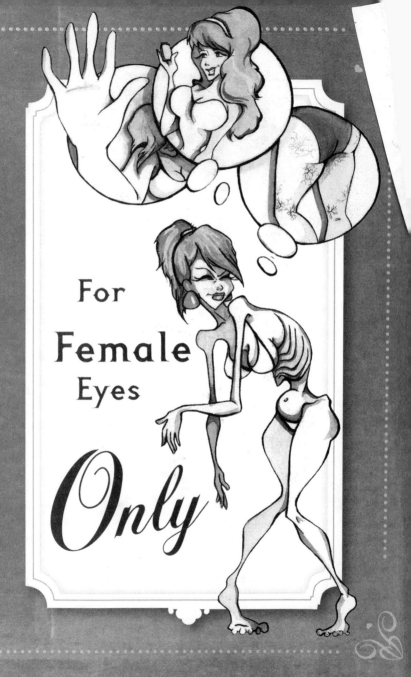

My Five-Day Diet...
That Only Lasted
Three

*O*h my God, you won't believe it! I lost a hundred pounds last night while I was sleeping! Oh no, wait, I fell asleep watching *America's Next Top Model* and thought that girl was me. Oops. Look, I know it's only been three days, but throw me a freakin' bone. At least let me start to see Elle Macpherson's cheekbones on my face. The word *diet*, by the way, stands for "I Died because I couldn't Eat It!"

No wonder this diet I'm on comes from doctors. It only lasts five days because then they have to check you in for a heart attack, rage issues, or passing out brought on by abnormal intake of dry toast and beets. But I'm excited about day four; I get no bread at all and dessert is sucking on ice cubes to prevent dehydration! I figure by four o'clock I should start to see Big Macs driving next to me in traffic, or chili dog friends coming over for a visit. And then after my cup of carrots and one bare weenie, I'll be off to bed with a headache, anger issues, delusions, and no energy. P.S. I'm so malnourished I can't even remember my old jean size, so how will I even know if this diet worked?! Good night, my little ice cream sandwiches . . .

Jennifer Love Hewitt

You're So Vain...
You Probably
Think This Varicose
Is About You

It was a gorgeous day, a perfect short, silky sundress kind of day. The kind of day when construction workers whistle at your very existence and you don't want to give them the "I am a woman" finger as usual. I was in my closet enjoying the delicious search for the perfect sandals, when I saw them—my great-grandmother's legs attached to my body. Why on Earth did I look eighty from the thighs down? I thought it was bad lighting (you know, the varicose lighting often found at Ikea . . . or not). How was I going to explain this to my summer wardrobe? How was I going to explain to my twenty-nine-year-old body that from the thighs up I had obviously not gotten the memo that I am aging? Why didn't *Cosmo* ever write about this happening? Forget "How to Do Your Best Friend's Guy" and horoscopes . . . Why had no one ever told me that the bubble in which we exist could burst at any moment? What was this and why?

As I did some asking, in between sending myself "you're still attractive" text messages, I found out that it happens to a lot of people. Didn't help me much, but misery loves company. I am starting to deal on a normal level now with my vain problem—pun intended. But where do I go from here? I mean, we don't get younger. Soon the varicose veins will be joined by other things: saggy boobs, wrinkles, and hair on my face. Yes, I did just say HAIR ON MY FACE. I could go on, but why? (P.S. I just sent myself another "you're still pretty" text.)

Jennifer Love Hewitt

Maybe I can make them a conversation piece?

"Hey, did you see my vein formation in the shape of Texas? Pretty cool, huh?" Or "Want to come over and play Connect the Veins?"

All right, I'm trying to be positive. I look at it this way—I have earned them. Here's the deal. We all have things that get us down. Love yourself anyway. The right people will love you for your heart, not your veins. So hold your head high, make those blue goddess lines your beauty mark, and make being vain a good thing.

The Day I Shot Cupid

Bitch,

Please

If ordering personality parts for a woman was like ordering food, it might sound like this: "I would like to have elegance as an appetizer; class, dignity, and sex appeal as my main course, with a side of great legs; and for dessert, a little bitch, please!"

Yes, I did just order a little bit of bitch. From this point on, *bitch* will be a good word, and for us, a compliment. It's that little bit of feisty that we may need to use every now and then. And even if the "bitch" is never used, just by carrying it inside, you will have an inner strength that will keep people from messing with you.

Sometimes you *have* to be a bitch. It will keep girls from pushing you too far and stop men from thinking you are a pushover. Now please, do not go and tell people that I, JLH, told you it was okay to be a bitch, but it is okay to have a little bit of bitch inside. So use it! Let your man know he will have to work (in a good way) to be with such a great woman. And that, if needed, your little friend "bitch" will come in and finish the conversation. And to "those types of women"—you know, the ones who seem to awaken even the smallest, quietest bitch—let 'er rip! They will be shocked and they will back down. I repeat, your inner bitch isn't to be used for bad, only the special moments when you need her. I may never say this again, but go ahead, ladies . . . BE A BITCH!!!

The Day I Shot Cupid

It was a strange day in my life, the day my bikini photo was plastered all over every magazine and Internet site imaginable. I found myself consumed with asking, "Why me?" I'm a nice person. I haven't harmed anyone. I honestly didn't get it. And what would other women think watching one of their own get attacked in this way? I finally came to the conclusion that it would be a very small, although painful, moment in my long existence. I would leave it in the past and move on. By the way, the whole situation totally made me hungry.

Fat, and
Not with a PH

hy do people need to comment? Did my supposed fat tell you how stupid you look in that color? Or how hard it is for me to listen to that ridiculous noise you call a laugh? No. My supposed fat sat right here in this little black dress, quietly drinking its margarita, waiting for the food it ordered. OH, I BET YOU LOVE THAT! FOOD. THAT'S RIGHT, I SAID FOOD! Food that might add to the fat you mentioned earlier when you drove your large stake into the tiny part of my heart that stores all of its self-confidence, but don't dare deprive me of it because I will get angry. And a hungry, upset, so-called fat person isn't pretty coming at you in a dark parking lot in her car.

I take a deep breath and realize that maybe you have the problem. Maybe you feel like you have to comment on my weight because you have your own worries. And suddenly I want to share with you a brief bite of my tasty morsels instead of shoving your face in them. I heard someone say once that a world without men would be a bunch of fat, happy women with no crime. So come on, let's pretend there is no one to impress for a moment. Stop being catty, grab a fork, and share my little bit of tasty heaven, and bite by low-calorie bite, take the world on tomorrow.

Jennifer Love Hewitt

OMG I'M

remember when I was twelve years old: my birthday wish was to be thirty. It just seemed that all the women I knew or looked up to always got cooler at thirty. It's when the girl finally sits to the side and the woman gets to take over. It's when you are no longer afraid to have a real opinion on that, want more for yourself than just the "okay for now" guy, and can look at yourself and actually like what you see.

On my thirtieth birthday, I felt like a new me, so free and ready to show what I was made of. I decided to spend my day paying homage to one of the greatest women we all know, Audrey Hepburn. I had breakfast at Tiffany's, lunch with my girlfriends, wore a tiara all day, and had the most fabulous party that left me dancing 'til 5 a.m.! It was glorious! I challenge us all to make every birthday as wonderful as thirty. Hold on to that "I have arrived" feeling, spend your birthdays paying homage to your favorite female icons, and remember, every year we get better. Here are a few things I have been doing for myself in my thirtieth year. No matter what age you are, you might want to give these a try.

1. Every day, look in the mirror and find ten things you like (you must say them out loud).

2. Every night before bed, find five things you think are sexy about

Jennifer Love Hewitt

yourself (that's right, say those out loud, too).

3. Sleep in sexy lingerie, not for him, but you. (Sleep naked for him.)

4. And my favorite, take a bath every night with a tiara on. It really does make you feel like a queen.

If you don't like these, come up with your own, but spend time on yourself and you will like the results.

The Day I Shot Cupid

Be Polite,
It's Cellulite

t starts off gently, a reminder to have one less french fry. A friendly, subtle "Hey there, you're no longer sixteen." A tiny, inconvenient, unimportant, barely noticeable, completely controllable bump. Misplaced cell or tissue, if you will. You don't even think to mention it over a girls' lunch because it will be gone after a forty-five-minute session on the treadmill. But then you wake up, two months later, after 150 hours on the treadmill, two weeks of sucking on ice, and eighteen massages for that little cell/misplaced tissue problem. And suddenly it hits you—it ain't a houseguest, it's here to stay. Your bathing suits have skirts on them. Your once string bikini is now surf trunks and a rash guard. You suddenly are very sensitive to sunlight and can only tan alone and at home. Department stores have seen what lurks under your jeans and have invented shorts—tight, skin-colored, cut-off-the-blood-supply shorts—meant to make you feel extremely secure when worn under your dresses and skinny jeans. Except you are getting no blood to your brain to make you feel secure. And now you waddle. They are so tight. You waddle over to the mirror and you tell yourself one last time that it's only a matter of days before this nightmare ends. Let's stop the insanity! (Thanks, Susan Powter.)

It is what it is. "Be polite, it's cellulite." Lots of women have it! A lot, a little, surface, deep, butt, thighs, whatever. The only personal victory I had was finding out and seeing with my own eyes that models have it. Yeah, perfect people are just like us! Let's all have a celly parade! Walk in bikinis and invite people to bring tomatoes to throw at our cottage cheese!

The Day I Shot Cupid

And the shorts from those Einsteins at the Spanx company have saved our lives. They should have their own day. Spanx Day! Don't shoot the messenger, but put on those shorts and learn to waddle!

Jennifer Love Hewitt

W.O.R.T.H.

(Women Over
Relationships That Hurt)

WORTH: The quality within a person that renders him or her worthy of respect.

This is a struggle I personally deal with. Worth. How to feel worth it. To be worthy. When I was thinking of the word, it hit me. Maybe those of us who struggle with this concept need to form a club, a secret society of women, who need to learn to feel worth it. And maybe we can do it by healing from the relationships that made us feel worthless. So we will form the Worth Club, Women Over Relationships That Hurt. Instead of constantly not feeling worthy and wondering why fulfillment is not found in new relationships, we will do inner work, which is really different for each person, to heal *ourselves* before moving into the next relationship. Here are a few steps that I think work.

1. First, figure out who or what made you feel unworthy. Accept your part, and what's not in your control, let go of.

2. Second, get a book on self-esteem, serious or funny, and actually read it, probably more than once.

3. Third, know that until you can believe that you are worthy of love from yourself, you can't and won't accept it from others. And when you feel that you are a truly worthy person, no relationship can actually break you.

To join this club, just be honest with yourself. Ask the person in the mirror to help you feel worthy, and then do your inner work. I think you are worth it.

Jennifer Love Hewitt

The Perfect Date,
Batteries Included

*O*h, the days of steamy novels, daydreams, and endless satisfaction with our dream man . . . Remember when a rabbit was a cute, fluffy animal that taught you responsibility? Not anymore. Samantha on *Sex and the City* proved that a good vibrator is as important as a toothbrush. The rabbit is an extremely well-sold vibrator that the modern woman packs before her undergarments. Our dream man is even threatened by the relationship between a gal and her AA Energizers. But here's the thing— sometimes a girl wants a quick "wham bam thank you ma'am" without all the perfume and fanfare, just like men and a *Playboy* centerfold. If she's single, it can keep her slutless and disease-free. If she's partnered, it can be used as a spice-up tool for even the most perfect relationships. And other times, it's just a way to express your naughty self without feeling like you need someone else for everything. Remember, it knows exactly what you need, doesn't talk back, shuts off when you say so, doesn't want anything in return, and can't kiss and tell. For those who are modest, name that little sucker and from now on tell people you are having a hot night with "Brad." Then go home, grab a glass of cabernet, and turn him on . . . wink, wink.

Jennifer Love Hewitt

Women wish to be loved not because
they are pretty, or good, or well bred,
or graceful, or intelligent, but because
they are themselves.

—Henri Frédéric Amiel
(1821–1881),
Swiss philosopher,
poet, critic

Fun

Little

Extras

10 Things to Do Before a Date

1. Always buy a new top or dress (it will make you feel like a million bucks).

2. Spray tan is a must.

3. Vagazzle it! (Not for him, for you!)

4. Eat a little snack so you don't eat like a Discovery Channel animal.

5. Listen to great music as you get ready. (Go, Beyoncé!)

6. Get a professional blowout (so you can do the slo-mo hair flip!).

7. Always get a mani-pedi. (Trust me, men love this!)

8. When you do last looks in the mirror, always check the back, too.

9. Remember, cleavage isn't cheap, it's gorgeous. (Show it off!)

10. Have a long conversation with yourself (this is not a marriage, it's a first date!).

Jennifer Love Hewitt

10 Things NOT to Do Before a Date

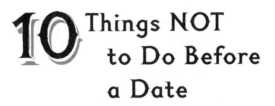

1. Don't watch romantic comedies (it won't be that amazing).

2. Don't try to check his criminal record online (wait 'til date number four).

3. Don't go slutty (guys do like girls with class).

4. Don't get tipsy to calm nerves.

5. Don't write "Mrs. _____" over and over on a piece of paper.

6. Don't ask other girls (except your BFFs) how you look. (Sorry, but they will lie.)

7. Don't take a diuretic; you will pee all night long.

8. Don't call six times to confirm. Only once. (That's just you afraid of getting stood up!)

9. Don't get on the scale; there isn't enough time to change it.

10. Don't worry if he's fifteen minutes late.

Jennifer Love Hewitt

5 Things He Should Say on a Date

1. You're hilarious.

2. You have beautiful eyes.

3. Let's do this again sometime.

4. Order what you want, dinner is on me.

5. Your friends didn't do you justice in the beauty department.

5 Things You Should NOT Say on a Date

1. I can see us spending the rest of our lives together.

2. You looked thinner in your photo.

3. I love the way you chew.

4. My last boyfriend . . .

5. I'm not so good at relationships.

 10 Hard-Core Truths About Men

This information was not fun to learn, but once you know these things, it all gets easier to deal with.

1. Men will always look. (It's animalistic; they have to check out girls.)

2. They don't always want to know what we are feeling. (They do tune us out.)

3. Men don't love to spoon or cuddle. (They'll do it, but they don't like it.)

4. They don't have a type of woman. (Guys who say, "Oh, she's not my type . . ." are liars. A man's type is a woman who is willing.)

5. They have to succeed in business and have to be supported in their dreams. (Encourage him to become who he wants to be. He will love you for it.)

6. Men don't always want undying adoration. (It puts pressure on them to keep up with the compliments.)

7. They will never give us exactly what we need in love (but a good one will try).

8. They will never understand our relationships with our moms (two women, too scary).

9. They can't read our minds. (We want them to, but they can't.)

Jennifer Love Hewitt

10. Men don't believe in romance.
    (It's not in their nature. They will
    learn it for you, but it's not
    something they believe in.)

The Day I Shot Cupid

What a Man
Should Know

- How to pick a diamond.

- How to make breakfast.

- How to pick a great bottle of wine.

- How to talk to our grandmothers.

- How to win over our moms.

- How to read a map.

- At least three ways to save a life.

- To always have a coat for you.

- How to ask for directions.

- How to be okay with needing a woman.

- When to listen.

- When to just shut up and kiss you.

The Day I Shot Cupid

What a Woman Should Know

- When not to be emotional.

- How to choose her battles.

- How to cook at least ten different meals.

- How to throw a dinner party.

- When to break out the sexy lingerie.

- When to just listen.

- When to not be the good girl.

- When to just let him zone out on video games, his computer, or phone.

- How to pick up the bill without asking (it's okay, it's 2010).

- How to trust him.

- When to let him control the day or situation.

- When to just shut up and kiss him.

The Day I Shot Cupid

What Does Love Mean?

A group of professional people posed this question to a group of four- to eight-year-olds: "What does love mean?" The answers they got were broader and deeper than anyone could have imagined:

"When my grandmother got arthritis, she couldn't bend over and paint her toenails anymore. So my grandfather does it for her all the time, even when his hands got arthritis too. That's love."

—*Rebecca, age 8*

"When somebody loves you, the way they say your name is different. You just know that your name is safe in their mouth."

—Billy, age 4

"Love is what makes you smile when you're tired."

—Terri, age 4

"Love is what's in the room with you at Christmas if you stop opening presents and listen."

—Bobby, age 7

"If you want to learn to love better, you should start with a friend who you hate."

—Nikka, age 6

"Love is when you tell a guy you like his shirt, then he wears it every day."

—Noelle, age 7

The Day I Shot Cupid

"Love is like a little old woman and a little old man who are still friends even after they know each other so well."

—Tommy, age 6

"Love is when Mommy sees Daddy smelly and sweaty and still says he is handsomer than Robert Redford."

—Chris, age 7

"When you love somebody, your eyelashes go up and down and little stars come out of you."

—Karen, age 7

Jennifer Love Hewitt

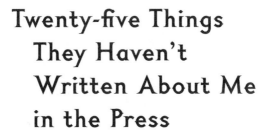

Twenty-five Things They Haven't Written About Me in the Press

1. I collect miniature old books.

2. I love office supplies (they get me all hot and bothered).

3. I secretly want to be BFF with LC (Lauren Conrad).

4. I'm really bad with computers.

5. I like margaritas with a splash of Sprite.

6. I love boxing (just to watch).

7. I love to clean my house.

8. I'm crazy about classic cars.

9. I read my horoscope every day.

10. Journey is my favorite rock band. (Met Steve Perry—almost passed out!)

11. My favorite holiday is Christmas.

12. I love to have game nights with my friends.

13. Cooking is my favorite thing to do (I make great cupcakes)!

14. I love to sleep in boys' underwear (not just any boy's).

15. I'm obsessed with using Purell hand sanitizer.

Jennifer Love Hewitt

16. My mom and I actually do a "Happy Dance" when there is good news.

17. I have to wear a funny "B-day Hat" every year on my birthday.

18. I really want to have children one day.

19. My feelings do get hurt when they say mean things about me or people I care about in the press.

20. I'm afraid of big birds (not the yellow *Sesame Street* kind).

21. Sour candies are my weakness.

22. I'm afraid of horror movies (I know I've been in some, but I still get scared).

The Day I Shot Cupid

23. I love to make scrapbooks
(just call me Martha).

24. I love monkeys.

25. I'm scared to speak in public.

You should make up your own list. It's a fun exercise!

Jennifer Love Hewitt

So It Comes to an End

t's only fitting that I end this book where I started. I am back in Cabo four years later, with a lot of water and romance under the bridge. So let's recap. I came here the first time with a broken heart, my girlfriends, and an idea for this book. Since then, I've dated a little, had a boyfriend, gotten engaged, had a fiancé, planned a wedding, had to say good-bye and ended up not getting married, am still storing a wedding dress in my closet (ouch!), grieved, turned thirty, laughed, cried, and finally finished this book! Where am I now? Really happy! A happiness that feels real and long-lasting, a new set of the most amazing girlfriends, lots of memories, and, what do you know, a new boyfriend! I've learned a lot about relationships, love, and myself. I hope you, too, will find happiness and joy. What's next for me in this slightly wounded, yet hopeful heart? I don't know, neither do you, and that is what's truly beautiful.

—JLH

Jennifer Love Hewitt

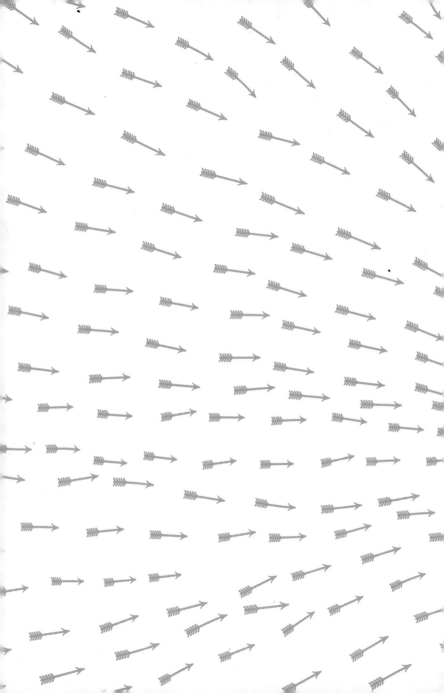